NURTURING ADD (ATTENTION DEFICIT DISORDER)

Understanding, Treating, and Healing Attention Deficit Disorder

NANCY JUDY

COPYRIGHT

TABLE OF CONTENTS

ABOUT THE BOOK

Welcome to "Nurturing ADD: Embracing Strengths, Overcoming Challenges." This book is a comprehensive guide and empowering narrative designed to support individuals living with Attention Deficit Disorder (ADD). Through practical strategies, personal anecdotes, and insightful advice, this book aims to foster understanding, empowerment, and resilience in navigating the complexities of ADD.

ADD, or Attention Deficit Disorder, is a neurodevelopmental condition characterized by difficulties in sustaining attention, organizing tasks, and managing impulses. However, it's crucial to recognize that ADD also brings unique strengths such as creativity, hyperfocus, and adaptability. This book delves into the multifaceted aspects of ADD, offering a deeper understanding of its impact on daily life and providing insights into how individuals can harness their innate abilities.

1. Embracing Neurodiversity: Central to this book is the celebration of neurodiversity. It encourages readers to embrace their unique cognitive styles, recognizing that ADD is a part of their identity rather than a limitation. Through personal stories and modern language, the book empowers individuals to cultivate self-acceptance and build confidence in their capabilities.

2. Practical Strategies: From managing time and organizing tasks to improving focus and reducing impulsivity, "Nurturing ADD" offers practical tools for everyday challenges. It provides actionable advice on creating supportive environments, establishing routines, and utilizing technology and organizational aids effectively.

3. Navigating Life's Challenges: Addressing common struggles such as procrastination, forgetfulness, and clutter, the book guides readers through strategies to overcome these hurdles.

Through storytelling elements and practical examples, it illustrates how individuals with ADD can achieve balance, enhance productivity, and thrive in various domains of life.

4. Advocacy and Awareness: The book advocates for greater awareness of ADD, challenging misconceptions and promoting inclusive practices in education, workplaces, and communities. It encourages readers to become advocates for themselves and others, fostering a supportive environment that values diversity and empowers individuals with ADD to reach their full potential.

"Nurturing ADD: Embracing Strengths, Overcoming Challenges" is more than just a book; it's a companion on the journey of understanding and living with ADD. It empowers readers to nurture their strengths, navigate challenges with resilience, and advocate for a more inclusive and supportive society. Whether you're living with ADD, supporting someone who is, or simply seeking to learn more, this book offers valuable insights and practical guidance for embracing neurodiversity and thriving in a world that celebrates individuality.

INTRODUCTION

In the realm of mental health and neurological conditions, Attention-Deficit/Hyperactivity Disorder (ADHD) stands as a complex yet often misunderstood phenomenon. More than just a label, ADHD profoundly impacts individuals across various facets of life, influencing how they learn, work, and relate to others. This introductory exploration seeks to set a compassionate stage for understanding ADHD, highlighting the critical need for personalized treatment and empathetic support.

ADHD manifests uniquely in each individual, challenging traditional notions of attention and behavior. It's crucial to recognize that ADHD isn't simply about "difficulty focusing" or "being hyperactive"; it encompasses a spectrum of cognitive and behavioral traits that can vary widely in intensity and expression. By setting this stage, we invite a nuanced understanding that moves beyond stereotypes and embraces the diversity of experiences within the ADHD community.

A holistic approach to ADHD involves acknowledging its multifaceted nature. It extends beyond diagnostic labels to encompass the individual's entire life context — their strengths, challenges, and personal aspirations. This perspective encourages us to view ADHD not as a limitation but as a unique cognitive profile that shapes how individuals navigate the world. By adopting this holistic lens, we can foster environments that nurture growth, resilience, and self-acceptance.

Central to compassionate care for ADHD is the recognition that one size does not fit all. Effective treatment goes beyond medication to include personalized strategies tailored to an individual's specific needs and circumstances. This may involve therapeutic interventions, educational accommodations, lifestyle adjustments, and support networks that empower individuals to thrive in their daily lives. By emphasizing personalized approaches, we honor the diversity of experiences within the ADHD community and promote outcomes that are meaningful and sustainable.

Personal narratives offer a powerful means of bridging understanding and empathy. By sharing stories of individuals living with ADHD — their triumphs, challenges, and everyday realities — we cultivate a deeper connection with readers. These stories illuminate the human side of ADHD, revealing the resilience, creativity, and unique perspectives that often accompany this condition. Through storytelling, we not only educate but also inspire compassion and solidarity within our communities.

Navigating ADHD requires a modern approach that integrates contemporary insights with practical guidance. This includes leveraging current research, understanding neurodiversity, and promoting inclusive language that respects individual experiences. Practical advice can range from organizational tips and time management strategies to advocating for ADHD-friendly environments in schools and workplaces. By equipping individuals and caregivers with actionable advice, we empower them to navigate ADHD with confidence and competence.

In conclusion, embracing a compassionate and holistic approach to understanding ADHD is not just about awareness — it's about fostering an environment where individuals feel seen, supported, and valued for who they are. By amplifying personal stories, advocating for personalized care, and embracing modern perspectives, we can create a more inclusive and empathetic society where everyone has the opportunity to thrive.

CHAPTER 1

THE ORIGINS OF ATTENTION DEFICIT DISORDER

Tracing the Historical Roots of ADHD Diagnosis and Treatment

The journey to understanding Attention-Deficit/Hyperactivity Disorder (ADHD) is a fascinating exploration that spans centuries. The condition we now recognize as ADHD has undergone numerous transformations in terminology, perception, and treatment approaches.

The earliest recorded observations of behaviors resembling ADHD date back to the late 18th century. Sir Alexander Crichton, a Scottish physician, described children with an "inability to attend with a necessary degree of constancy to any one object." His work, "An Inquiry into the Nature and Origin of Mental Derangement," published in 1798, highlighted the challenges of inattention and hyperactivity long before the term "ADHD" was coined.

Fast forward to the early 20th century, where the focus shifted towards understanding children's behavioral and cognitive patterns. In 1902, British pediatrician Sir George Frederic Still delivered lectures on what he referred to as "an abnormal defect of moral control in children." His observations included impulsivity, inattention, and hyperactivity, laying the groundwork for future research and diagnostic criteria.

The mid-20th century brought significant advancements in the conceptualization and treatment of ADHD. In the 1930s, Dr. Charles Bradley discovered that the stimulant Benzedrine had a paradoxical calming effect on hyperactive children. This serendipitous finding marked the beginning of pharmacological treatment for ADHD.

In the 1960s and 1970s, the term "hyperkinetic reaction of childhood" emerged, emphasizing hyperactivity as a core feature. However, by the 1980s, the Diagnostic and Statistical Manual of Mental Disorders (DSM-III) redefined the condition as "Attention-Deficit Disorder (ADD)," recognizing inattention as a separate dimension. The DSM-III-R, published in 1987, further refined the criteria, introducing the term "Attention-Deficit/Hyperactivity Disorder (ADHD)," which acknowledged the spectrum of inattention, hyperactivity, and impulsivity.

Challenging Misconceptions About ADHD as a Genetic "Illness"

One of the most pervasive misconceptions about ADHD is the notion that it is purely a genetic "illness." While genetic factors do play a significant role in the development of ADHD, it is essential to understand that ADHD is a complex neurodevelopmental condition influenced by a combination of genetic, environmental, and neurobiological factors.

Research has shown that ADHD tends to run in families, suggesting a genetic component. Studies involving twins have demonstrated that if one twin has ADHD, the likelihood of the other twin also having the condition is significantly higher. However, it is not solely genetics that determine the presence of ADHD. Environmental influences, such as prenatal exposure to alcohol or tobacco, low birth weight, and early exposure to lead, can contribute to the development of ADHD symptoms.

Moreover, the brain's structure and function play a critical role in ADHD. Neuroimaging studies have revealed differences in the size and activity of certain brain regions involved in attention, impulse control, and executive function. These findings underscore that ADHD is rooted in the brain's neurobiology rather than being a simple behavioral issue.

The Role of Environmental Stressors in the Development of ADHD Symptoms

While genetics and neurobiology provide a foundation for understanding ADHD, environmental stressors can significantly impact the severity and manifestation of symptoms. Environmental stressors encompass a wide range of factors, from family dynamics and socioeconomic status to educational environments and exposure to trauma.

Family Dynamics and Parenting

The family environment plays a crucial role in shaping a child's development and behavior. Children with ADHD often face challenges in family dynamics, such as inconsistent parenting, high levels of conflict, and lack of structure. While ADHD is not caused by poor parenting, these factors can exacerbate symptoms and make it more difficult for children to manage their behaviors.

Consider the story of Sarah, a young girl diagnosed with ADHD at the age of seven. Sarah's parents struggled to establish consistent routines and discipline, leading to frequent conflicts and emotional turmoil. The lack of structure in Sarah's home environment contributed to her difficulties in managing impulsivity and staying focused. However, with the help of a family therapist, Sarah's parents learned strategies to create a more supportive and structured environment, significantly improving Sarah's ability to cope with her symptoms.

Socioeconomic Status

Socioeconomic status (SES) can also influence the development and severity of ADHD symptoms. Children from low-income families may face additional stressors, such as limited access to healthcare, educational resources, and stable housing. These stressors can compound the challenges associated with ADHD, making it harder for children to succeed academically and socially.

For example, consider the story of Marcus, a bright and energetic boy growing up in an economically disadvantaged neighborhood. Marcus's family struggled to afford his medication and therapy, and his school lacked the resources to provide individualized support. Despite these challenges, Marcus's determination and the support of a dedicated teacher helped him find alternative strategies to manage his symptoms, such as mindfulness exercises and after-school tutoring programs.

Educational Environments

The educational environment can significantly impact children with ADHD. Traditional classroom settings, which often emphasize sustained attention and self-regulation, can be particularly challenging for students with ADHD. Without appropriate accommodations, these students may struggle to keep up with their peers and experience feelings of frustration and inadequacy.

Consider the story of Emma, a high school student with ADHD. Emma found it challenging to focus during long lectures and often felt overwhelmed by the demands of homework and exams. However, with the support of her school's special education team, Emma received accommodations such as extended test time and access to a quiet study space. These adjustments allowed Emma to thrive academically and develop confidence in her abilities.

Exposure to Trauma

Exposure to trauma, such as abuse, neglect, or witnessing violence, can have a profound impact on the development of ADHD symptoms. Traumatic experiences can disrupt brain development and impair emotional regulation, making it more difficult for individuals to manage impulsivity and attention.

For instance, consider the story of Jack, a young boy who witnessed domestic violence in his home. Jack's trauma contributed to his difficulties in focusing and controlling his impulses. Through trauma-informed therapy and a supportive school environment, Jack learned coping strategies to manage his symptoms and heal from his past experiences.

Incorporating Storytelling Elements, Modern Language, and Practical Advice

Understanding the origins and development of ADHD requires a blend of historical context, modern insights, and practical advice. By incorporating storytelling elements, we can humanize the experiences of individuals with ADHD and offer relatable perspectives.

Practical Advice for Families and Caregivers

1. Create Structure and Consistency: Establishing predictable routines and clear expectations can help children with ADHD feel more secure and capable. Use visual schedules, checklists, and reminders to support daily activities.

2. Promote Positive Reinforcement: Reinforce desired behaviors with praise and rewards. Positive reinforcement can motivate children with ADHD and build their self-esteem.

3. Collaborate with Educators: Work closely with teachers and school staff to develop individualized education plans (IEPs) or 504 plans that provide necessary accommodations and support.

4. Seek Professional Help: Consider seeking the guidance of mental health professionals, such as psychologists, psychiatrists, or therapists, who specialize in ADHD. They can provide valuable insights and strategies for managing symptoms.

5. Encourage Physical Activity: Regular physical activity can improve attention, mood, and overall well-being. Encourage activities that your child enjoys, such as sports, dancing, or outdoor play.

6. Practice Mindfulness and Relaxation Techniques: Mindfulness exercises, such as deep breathing, meditation, and yoga, can help individuals with ADHD develop better self-regulation and reduce stress.

The origins of Attention-Deficit/Hyperactivity Disorder are deeply rooted in a rich history of observation, research, and evolving understanding. By challenging misconceptions and recognizing the role of environmental stressors, we can approach ADHD with greater compassion and insight. Through personalized treatment, supportive environments, and practical strategies, individuals with ADHD can navigate their unique challenges and harness their strengths, leading fulfilling and empowered lives.

CHAPTER 2

NEW DIAGNOSTIC PROCEDURES AND EVALUATIONS FOR ADHD

In recent years, advances in diagnostic tools and assessments have revolutionized the way we identify and understand Attention Deficit Hyperactivity Disorder (ADHD). These cutting-edge approaches are transforming our ability to diagnose ADHD with greater accuracy, paving the way for early detection and timely intervention. This essay explores these innovative diagnostic procedures, underscores evidence-based practices for diagnosing ADHD across different age groups, and highlights the critical importance of early identification and intervention.

Exploring Cutting-Edge Diagnostic Tools and Assessments

Traditional methods of diagnosing ADHD have largely relied on clinical interviews, behavioral checklists, and self-reported symptoms. While these methods remain valuable, they often lack the precision needed to capture the multifaceted nature of ADHD. Recent technological advancements are bridging this gap, providing more nuanced and comprehensive evaluations.

One of the most promising developments is the use of neuroimaging techniques. Functional MRI (fMRI) and positron emission tomography (PET) scans offer insights into the brain activity and structural differences associated with ADHD. These imaging tools allow clinicians to observe areas of the brain involved in attention, impulse control, and executive functioning. For example, research has shown that individuals with ADHD often exhibit reduced activity in the prefrontal cortex, the region responsible for regulating behavior and decision-making.

Another cutting-edge tool is the Quantitative Electroencephalography (qEEG). This technique measures electrical activity in the brain, identifying atypical patterns associated with ADHD. By analyzing brain wave frequencies, qEEG can provide objective data that supports clinical observations, enhancing the accuracy of ADHD diagnosis.

Beyond neuroimaging, digital assessments are becoming increasingly prevalent. Computerized Continuous Performance Tests (CPTs) assess attention and impulse control by measuring an individual's response to specific tasks over a period of time. These tests can identify subtle deficits in attention and highlight patterns indicative of ADHD. Additionally, digital platforms and apps are being developed to monitor behavioral symptoms in real-time, offering a more dynamic and holistic view of an individual's functioning in daily life.

Highlighting Evidence-Based Approaches Across Age Groups

Diagnosing ADHD accurately requires evidence-based approaches tailored to different age groups. Children, adolescents, and adults each present unique challenges and considerations in the diagnostic process.

For young children, early diagnosis is crucial yet challenging due to the natural variability in behavior and development. Clinicians often rely on multi-informant reports, gathering information from parents, teachers, and caregivers to form a comprehensive picture of the child's behavior across settings. Play-based assessments and observational techniques also play a significant role. For instance, structured play sessions can reveal difficulties in sustaining attention, following instructions, and regulating emotions.

In adolescents, the diagnostic process must account for the developmental changes and social pressures characteristic of this age group. Adolescents may be more aware of their symptoms and better able to articulate their experiences. Self-report questionnaires, alongside reports from parents and teachers, are commonly used. Additionally, neuropsychological tests that assess executive functions, working memory, and attention can provide objective data to support a diagnosis.

For adults, ADHD diagnosis often involves retrospective assessments of childhood behavior and current functioning. Many adults with ADHD may not have been diagnosed in childhood, leading to a complex clinical presentation. Structured clinical interviews, self-report scales, and informant reports from partners or close relatives are essential components. Furthermore, assessing co-occurring conditions such as anxiety, depression, and substance use disorders is crucial, as these can complicate the diagnostic picture.

Importance of Early Detection and Intervention

Early detection and intervention for ADHD are paramount in improving long-term outcomes. When ADHD is identified and addressed promptly, individuals are better equipped to manage their symptoms, develop coping strategies, and achieve their full potential.

Early intervention begins with awareness and education. Parents, educators, and healthcare providers must be informed about the signs and symptoms of ADHD to facilitate timely referrals for assessment. Public health campaigns and educational programs can play a vital role in raising awareness and reducing the stigma associated with ADHD.

Once diagnosed, early intervention should encompass a multi-modal approach. Behavioral interventions, psychoeducation, and family support are essential components. Behavioral therapy, such as Parent-Child Interaction Therapy (PCIT) and Cognitive Behavioral Therapy (CBT), can help children develop self-regulation skills, improve social interactions, and reduce disruptive behaviors. In schools, individualized education plans (IEPs) and classroom accommodations ensure that students with ADHD receive the support they need to succeed academically and socially.

For adolescents and adults, early intervention may include skills training, vocational support, and psychotherapy. Learning organizational skills, time management, and stress reduction techniques can significantly enhance daily functioning and overall well-being. Support groups and peer networks provide valuable platforms for sharing experiences and strategies, fostering a sense of community and empowerment.

A Personal Journey

To illustrate the transformative impact of early detection and intervention, let's consider the story of Emily, a young girl diagnosed with ADHD at the age of seven. Emily's parents noticed early on that she had difficulty focusing on tasks, was frequently impulsive, and struggled with emotional regulation. Concerned about her academic performance and social interactions, they sought an evaluation from a pediatric neuropsychologist.

Through a comprehensive assessment involving behavioral observations, neuropsychological testing, and input from her teachers, Emily was diagnosed with ADHD. This early diagnosis allowed her family to access the necessary resources and support. Emily began receiving behavioral therapy to develop coping strategies and improve her social skills. Her school implemented an individualized education plan that included classroom accommodations, such as extended time for assignments and frequent breaks.

Over time, Emily's self-esteem and academic performance improved. She learned techniques to manage her impulsivity and developed strong organizational skills. With the support of her family, teachers, and therapists, Emily thrived. Her story exemplifies the positive outcomes that can result from early detection and intervention, highlighting the potential for individuals with ADHD to achieve their goals and lead fulfilling lives.

Practical Advice: Navigating the Diagnostic Process

For those navigating the diagnostic process, practical advice can help ensure a thorough and accurate assessment. Here are some key steps:

1. Seek a Qualified Professional: Consult with a specialist experienced in diagnosing ADHD, such as a child psychologist, psychiatrist, or neuropsychologist. Ensure they use evidence-based diagnostic tools and have a comprehensive understanding of ADHD.

2. Gather Comprehensive Information: Provide detailed information about the individual's behavior across different settings. This includes input from parents, teachers, and other caregivers for children, and self-reports for adolescents and adults.

3. Consider Co-Occurring Conditions: ADHD often co-occurs with other conditions, such as anxiety, depression, learning disabilities, and conduct disorders. A thorough assessment should screen for these conditions to inform an accurate diagnosis and comprehensive treatment plan.

4. Utilize Objective Measures: Incorporate objective assessments, such as neuropsychological tests, CPTs, and qEEG, to supplement clinical observations and self-reports. These tools can provide valuable data to support the diagnostic process.

5. Advocate for Early Intervention: If ADHD is diagnosed, seek early intervention services. Behavioral therapy, educational accommodations, and family support are critical components of a comprehensive treatment plan.

6. Educate and Empower: Educate yourself and your family about ADHD. Understanding the condition, its challenges, and strengths can foster a supportive and empowering environment.

The landscape of ADHD diagnosis is evolving, with cutting-edge tools and evidence-based approaches enhancing our ability to accurately identify and support individuals with ADHD. Early detection and intervention are crucial in improving outcomes, enabling individuals to develop coping strategies, achieve their potential, and lead fulfilling lives. By embracing these advances and promoting awareness, we can create a more inclusive and supportive society for individuals with ADHD.

CHAPTER 3

RECOGNIZING AND COPING WITH ADHD: A COMPREHENSIVE GUIDE

Attention-Deficit/Hyperactivity Disorder (ADHD) is a complex condition that affects individuals across their lifespan, presenting unique challenges that require tailored strategies for recognition and coping. This guide delves into the early signs and symptoms of ADHD in both children and adults, offers practical coping mechanisms for managing daily challenges, and promotes resilience and self-advocacy skills through engaging storytelling and actionable advice.

Recognizing Early Signs and Symptoms of ADHD

In Children

Recognizing ADHD in children often begins with observing behavioral patterns that deviate from developmental norms. Common signs include:

- Inattention: Children may struggle to focus on tasks, frequently make careless mistakes, or seem to daydream during conversations and activities.
- Hyperactivity: This can manifest as constant fidgeting, running or climbing in inappropriate situations, and an inability to stay seated or play quietly.
- Impulsivity: Impulsive behaviors include blurting out answers, interrupting others, and difficulty waiting for their turn in games or conversations.

For instance, consider the story of Emma, a spirited six-year-old who often finds herself daydreaming during class and jumping from one activity to another without finishing any. Her parents noticed her inability to sit still during dinner and her frequent outbursts when she had to wait her turn to speak. These early signs prompted them to seek a professional evaluation, leading to an ADHD diagnosis and the beginning of a supportive intervention plan.

In Adults

ADHD symptoms in adults can be more nuanced but still impactful. Signs may include:

- Disorganization: Difficulty managing time, tasks, and personal belongings.
- Restlessness: Feeling an internal sense of restlessness, which may or may not be physically apparent.
- Impulsivity: Making hasty decisions without considering long-term consequences, such as impulsive spending or job changes.
- Attention difficulties: Struggling to focus on tasks, especially those that are repetitive or require sustained attention.

Take John, a 35-year-old graphic designer who excelled in creative tasks but consistently missed deadlines and forgot important meetings. His tendency to impulsively switch projects and his chronic disorganization at home strained his professional and personal life. It wasn't until a friend suggested he might have ADHD that John sought an evaluation, leading to a diagnosis that helped him understand his challenges and seek appropriate support.

Coping Mechanisms for Managing ADHD-Related Challenges

Establishing Routines

One effective coping strategy for both children and adults with ADHD is establishing clear, consistent routines. Predictable schedules help reduce anxiety and increase productivity by providing structure. For children, visual schedules with pictures and charts can be particularly helpful, while adults may benefit from digital planners and reminder apps.

For example, Emma's parents created a colorful morning routine chart with pictures of brushing teeth, getting dressed, and packing her school bag. This visual aid helped Emma understand and follow her daily routine with fewer reminders, making mornings smoother for the whole family.

Mindfulness and Relaxation Techniques

Mindfulness practices, such as deep breathing, meditation, and yoga, can help individuals with ADHD manage stress and improve focus. These techniques encourage a greater awareness of thoughts and feelings, helping to reduce impulsivity and emotional reactivity.

John found that incorporating a daily meditation practice helped him feel more centered and less overwhelmed by his to-do list. He also took short breaks throughout his workday to practice deep breathing exercises, which helped him refocus and manage his restlessness.

Behavioral Therapy and Coaching

Behavioral therapy, particularly Cognitive Behavioral Therapy (CBT), can be highly effective for individuals with ADHD. CBT focuses on identifying and changing negative thought patterns and behaviors, improving emotional regulation, and developing practical coping skills.

In Emma's case, her therapist used CBT techniques to help her develop better impulse control and coping strategies for frustration. For adults like John, ADHD coaching can provide personalized support and accountability, helping them set realistic goals and develop strategies to achieve them.

Organizational Tools and Strategies

Using organizational tools can make a significant difference in managing ADHD symptoms. These tools include planners, to-do lists, and digital apps designed to track tasks and deadlines. Breaking tasks into smaller, manageable steps and setting specific deadlines can also help.

John started using a project management app to organize his tasks and set reminders for important deadlines. He also created a designated workspace at home, free from distractions, to help him stay focused during work hours.

Physical Activity and Healthy Lifestyle

Regular physical activity has been shown to improve focus, mood, and overall well-being for individuals with ADHD. Incorporating exercise into daily routines can help reduce hyperactivity and impulsivity.

Emma's parents enrolled her in a dance class, which provided an outlet for her energy and improved her ability to concentrate during school hours. John joined a local gym and started a morning workout routine, which helped him feel more energized and focused throughout the day.

Promoting Resilience and Self-Advocacy Skills

Building Self-Awareness

Self-awareness is the foundation of resilience and self-advocacy. Understanding one's strengths and challenges allows individuals with ADHD to develop effective coping strategies and advocate for their needs.

John's journey to self-awareness involved reflecting on his ADHD symptoms and how they impacted his life. By acknowledging his challenges with organization and time management, he could seek specific strategies and support to address these areas.

Developing Problem-Solving Skills

Teaching problem-solving skills empowers individuals with ADHD to navigate challenges independently. This involves breaking down problems into manageable steps, brainstorming potential solutions, and evaluating the outcomes.

Emma's therapist used problem-solving exercises to help her navigate social interactions at school. By role-playing different scenarios, Emma learned to identify appropriate responses and develop strategies for handling conflicts with peers.

Fostering a Supportive Environment

A supportive environment is crucial for promoting resilience. This includes creating a home and school environment that accommodates ADHD-related needs and encourages positive behavior.

Emma's teachers worked with her parents to implement accommodations such as extended time on tests and a quiet space for completing assignments. These adjustments helped Emma feel more confident and successful in her academic endeavors.

Encouraging Self-Advocacy

Self-advocacy involves teaching individuals with ADHD to understand their rights, communicate their needs, and seek appropriate accommodations and support. This skill is essential for navigating educational, professional, and social environments.

John learned to advocate for himself at work by having open conversations with his manager about his ADHD and the accommodations he needed to succeed. This included flexible deadlines and regular check-ins to ensure he stayed on track with his projects.

Practical Advice for Everyday Life

Time Management Tips

1. Use Timers and Alarms: Set timers for tasks to help stay on track and avoid hyperfocusing on one activity.

2. Prioritize Tasks: Identify the most important tasks for the day and focus on completing them first.

3. Break Tasks into Smaller Steps: Divide larger projects into smaller, more manageable tasks to reduce overwhelm.

Organizational Strategies

1. Create Designated Spaces: Designate specific areas for work, relaxation, and personal items to reduce clutter and distractions.

2. Use Visual Aids: Utilize color-coded folders, labels, and visual schedules to keep track of tasks and deadlines.

3. Implement a Filing System: Develop a simple filing system for important documents to ensure they are easily accessible.

Managing Impulsivity

1. Practice Mindfulness: Engage in mindfulness exercises to increase awareness of impulsive thoughts and actions.

2. Pause and Reflect: Before making decisions, take a moment to pause and consider the potential consequences.

3. Develop Healthy Outlets: Channel impulsive energy into productive activities such as exercise, hobbies, or creative pursuits.

Enhancing Focus

1. Eliminate Distractions: Create a distraction-free workspace by minimizing noise, organizing materials, and limiting access to digital devices.

2. Use Focus Techniques: Experiment with focus techniques such as the Pomodoro Technique, which involves working in short, focused bursts with regular breaks.

3. Seek Support: Collaborate with a coach or therapist to develop personalized strategies for improving focus and productivity.

Recognizing and coping with ADHD requires a multifaceted approach that encompasses early detection, practical coping mechanisms, and the development of resilience and self-advocacy skills. By integrating modern diagnostic tools, evidence-based strategies, and supportive interventions, individuals with ADHD can navigate their challenges and harness their unique strengths.

Through the stories of Emma and John, we see the power of early recognition, personalized support, and resilience-building in transforming lives. Whether through establishing routines, practicing mindfulness, or advocating for accommodations, these strategies empower individuals with ADHD to thrive in their personal, academic, and professional endeavors.

In embracing a holistic and compassionate approach to ADHD, we foster environments that value neurodiversity and promote the well-being and success of all individuals. By recognizing the unique experiences and needs of those with ADHD, we create a more inclusive and supportive society where everyone has the opportunity to reach their full potential.

CHAPTER 4

HUMANITARIAN, ECONOMIC, AND DIVERSITY ISSUES

The Societal Impact of ADHD: A Comprehensive Exploration of Humanitarian, Economic, and Diversity Issues

Attention-Deficit/Hyperactivity Disorder (ADHD) is not just a personal challenge; it reverberates through families, communities, and society at large. This narrative examines the societal impact of ADHD, highlighting the humanitarian, economic, and diversity issues it entails. By incorporating storytelling elements, modern language, and practical advice, this exploration aims to foster greater awareness and inclusivity for individuals with ADHD.

Examining the Societal Impact of ADHD

The Humanitarian Perspective: Lives Shaped by ADHD

ADHD affects millions of individuals worldwide, influencing their daily lives, relationships, and opportunities. For many, the journey with ADHD is fraught with misunderstandings and misconceptions. Parents may struggle to understand their child's erratic behavior, while adults may face challenges in maintaining jobs or relationships. These struggles can lead to a pervasive sense of frustration and self-doubt.

Consider the story of Emily, a bright young girl who could never seem to sit still in class. Her teachers labeled her as disruptive, and her peers avoided her due to her impulsivity. Emily's parents, unsure how to help, felt a mix of helplessness and guilt. It wasn't until a compassionate school counselor recognized the signs of ADHD that Emily received the support she needed. With proper interventions, Emily's potential began to shine through her challenges, transforming her life and easing the stress on her family.

Impact on Families: Navigating the ADHD Journey Together

Families of individuals with ADHD often face unique challenges. Parents may feel overwhelmed by their child's behavioral issues, leading to stress and strain within the household. Siblings might feel neglected as parents devote more time and resources to managing ADHD-related challenges. This dynamic can create a cycle of tension and misunderstanding within the family unit.

However, with proper education and support, families can learn to navigate these challenges together. For instance, family therapy can provide a space for open communication, helping each member understand ADHD and its impact. Support groups for parents offer a community of shared experiences, reducing feelings of isolation and providing practical advice.

Community Impact: The Ripple Effect of ADHD

The effects of ADHD extend beyond individuals and families, influencing communities at large. In educational settings, undiagnosed or unsupported ADHD can lead to academic underachievement, behavioral issues, and increased dropout rates. This not only affects the individual but also places additional strain on educational resources and staff.

Workplaces also feel the impact of ADHD. Employees with ADHD may struggle with time management, organization, and maintaining focus, leading to decreased productivity and higher turnover rates. However, with appropriate accommodations and an understanding work environment, individuals with ADHD can thrive and contribute significantly to their workplaces.

Addressing Economic Disparities in Access to ADHD Treatment and Support

The Cost of ADHD: Financial Burdens on Families and Society

The economic impact of ADHD is substantial, affecting both families and society. Families often bear the direct costs of diagnosis and treatment, which can include medical evaluations, therapy sessions, medication, and educational support services. For many, these expenses are prohibitive, particularly for those without adequate health insurance.

Consider the story of Marcus, a single father working two jobs to support his family. His son, Jamal, exhibits classic signs of ADHD, but the cost of a formal diagnosis and subsequent treatment is beyond Marcus's reach. As a result, Jamal's academic performance suffers, and his behavioral issues escalate, creating a vicious cycle of frustration and missed opportunities.

Economic Disparities: Access to Treatment and Support

Economic disparities significantly influence access to ADHD treatment and support. Low-income families often face barriers to obtaining a proper diagnosis and accessing effective interventions. This inequity perpetuates a cycle of disadvantage, as untreated ADHD can lead to poorer educational and employment outcomes, further entrenching economic hardship.

Communities of color and marginalized groups are disproportionately affected by these disparities. Systemic inequalities in healthcare, education, and socioeconomic status mean that children and adults from these communities are less likely to receive timely and adequate ADHD support. This highlights the urgent need for policies and programs that address these inequities and promote equal access to care.

Policy and Advocacy: Bridging the Gap

Addressing economic disparities in ADHD treatment requires concerted policy efforts and advocacy. Governments and healthcare systems must prioritize funding for mental health services, ensuring that all individuals, regardless of economic status, have access to the care they need. Schools can play a crucial role by implementing programs that identify and support students with ADHD, providing resources for both students and teachers.

Nonprofit organizations and community groups are also vital in bridging the gap. By offering subsidized services, educational workshops, and advocacy initiatives, these organizations can help alleviate the financial burden on families and promote greater awareness and understanding of ADHD.

Advocating for Greater Awareness and Inclusivity

The Role of Awareness: Shattering Stigma and Misconceptions

Awareness and education are key to creating an inclusive society for individuals with ADHD. Misunderstandings and stigma surrounding ADHD can lead to discrimination and social isolation, exacerbating the challenges faced by those with the condition. Public awareness campaigns and educational programs can help dispel myths and promote a more accurate understanding of ADHD.

Imagine the story of Carlos, a teenager with ADHD who was often labeled as lazy or unmotivated by his teachers. A school-wide awareness campaign about ADHD helped change this perception, leading to increased empathy and support from his peers and educators. As a result, Carlos felt more accepted and motivated to succeed academically.

Inclusivity in Diverse Backgrounds: Embracing Neurodiversity

ADHD affects individuals from all backgrounds, yet cultural differences can influence how ADHD is perceived and addressed. In some cultures, there may be stigma attached to mental health conditions, leading to reluctance in seeking diagnosis and treatment. Language barriers and lack of culturally competent healthcare providers further exacerbate these challenges.

Promoting inclusivity involves recognizing and respecting these cultural differences while advocating for equitable access to care. Healthcare providers must receive training in cultural competence to better understand and address the unique needs of diverse populations. Community outreach programs can bridge gaps by providing information and resources in multiple languages and culturally relevant formats.

Empowerment and Self-Advocacy: Building a Supportive Community

Empowering individuals with ADHD to advocate for themselves is crucial in promoting inclusivity and resilience. Self-advocacy involves understanding one's rights, recognizing personal strengths and challenges, and effectively communicating needs in various settings. This empowerment can lead to greater self-confidence and improved outcomes in education, employment, and social interactions.

Practical advice for self-advocacy includes:

- Education: Learning about ADHD and how it specifically affects you or your loved one is the first step. Understanding the condition helps in articulating needs and seeking appropriate accommodations.
- Communication: Developing effective communication skills to express challenges and request support is vital. This includes practicing assertiveness and clarity in both personal and professional contexts.
- Support Networks: Building a network of supportive individuals, including family, friends, educators, and healthcare providers, can provide encouragement and practical assistance. Joining ADHD support groups offers a sense of community and shared experiences.

Storytelling Elements: Bringing Experiences to Life

Personal Narratives: The Power of Shared Stories

Personal stories of individuals with ADHD can illuminate the diverse experiences and challenges faced, fostering empathy and understanding. These narratives highlight the resilience, creativity, and unique perspectives that often accompany ADHD.

Consider the story of Sarah, a successful entrepreneur who discovered her ADHD diagnosis in adulthood. Throughout her life, Sarah faced numerous challenges, including difficulty focusing, impulsive decisions, and struggles with time management. However, her ADHD also fueled her creativity and innovative thinking, which became key assets in her business. Sarah's journey of self-discovery and empowerment illustrates the transformative potential of understanding and embracing ADHD.

Fostering Inclusivity and Understanding

Using modern language that respects and acknowledges neurodiversity is crucial in fostering an inclusive environment. Terms like "neurodivergent" and "neurotypical" recognize the diversity of cognitive functioning and promote acceptance of different ways of thinking and processing information.

In educational and professional settings, adopting inclusive language and practices can create a supportive atmosphere for individuals with ADHD. This includes using person-first language (e.g., "person with ADHD" rather than "ADHD person") and implementing policies that accommodate diverse needs.

Practical Advice: Navigating ADHD in Daily Life

Educational Settings: Supporting Students with ADHD

In schools, teachers can support students with ADHD by implementing classroom accommodations and individualized education plans (IEPs). Strategies such as providing clear instructions, breaking tasks into manageable steps, and allowing for movement breaks can enhance learning and focus.

Workplace Strategies: Enhancing Productivity and Inclusion

Employers can create ADHD-friendly workplaces by offering flexible schedules, providing organizational tools, and fostering a culture of understanding. Encouraging open communication about ADHD can lead to better support and accommodations, ultimately benefiting both employees and the organization.

Daily Life: Managing ADHD Challenges

Individuals with ADHD can benefit from practical strategies to manage daily challenges. These include:

- Routine and Structure: Establishing consistent routines helps manage time and reduce forgetfulness.
- Technology Aids: Utilizing digital tools such as calendars, reminders, and task management apps can enhance organization and productivity.

- Mindfulness and Exercise: Incorporating mindfulness practices and regular physical activity can improve focus and emotional regulation.

The societal impact of ADHD is profound, touching on humanitarian, economic, and diversity issues. By examining these aspects through storytelling, modern language, and practical advice, we can foster greater awareness, empathy, and inclusivity for individuals with ADHD. Empowering individuals with ADHD, supporting their families, and advocating for equitable access to treatment and resources are essential steps toward creating a more understanding and inclusive society. Through these efforts, we can help individuals with ADHD realize their full potential and contribute meaningfully to their communities.

CHAPTER 5

UNDERSTANDING THE LINK BETWEEN ADHD AND ADD: A JOURNEY OF CLARITY AND COMPASSION

ADHD (Attention Deficit Hyperactivity Disorder) and ADD (Attention Deficit Disorder) are often used interchangeably, yet they represent distinct facets of a complex neurodevelopmental condition. This narrative seeks to clarify their relationship, explore common symptoms and challenges, and emphasize the importance of personalized care. By weaving storytelling elements, modern language, and practical advice, we aim to foster a deeper understanding and compassionate approach to these conditions.

Clarifying the Relationship Between ADD and ADHD

Historical Context and Evolution of Terminology

Historically, the term ADD was used to describe a subset of ADHD characterized by inattention without hyperactivity. In the 1980s, the Diagnostic and Statistical Manual of Mental Disorders (DSM) used ADD to refer to these symptoms, differentiating it from ADHD, which included hyperactivity and impulsivity. However, subsequent revisions of the DSM, particularly DSM-IV in 1994 and DSM-5 in 2013, consolidated these terms under the umbrella of ADHD, recognizing three primary presentations:

1. Predominantly Inattentive Presentation: Often referred to as ADD in casual language, this presentation is marked by significant inattention and distractibility without the hyperactivity and impulsivity seen in other forms of ADHD.

2. Predominantly Hyperactive-Impulsive Presentation: This presentation is characterized by hyperactivity and impulsivity without significant inattention.

3. Combined Presentation: Individuals exhibit both inattentive and hyperactive-impulsive symptoms.

Common Symptoms and Challenges

Symptoms Across Presentations

While ADHD and ADD share core symptoms of inattention, they differ in the presence of hyperactivity and impulsivity:

- Inattention: Difficulty sustaining attention, frequent careless mistakes, forgetfulness, and challenges in organizing tasks and activities.
- Hyperactivity: Fidgeting, restlessness, excessive talking, and an inability to stay seated or still.
- Impulsivity: Interrupting others, difficulty waiting for turns, and making hasty decisions without considering consequences.

Challenges in Daily Life

Individuals with ADHD or ADD face a range of challenges that impact various aspects of their lives:

- Academic and Occupational Struggles: Inattentiveness and disorganization can lead to underperformance in school or work, despite intellectual capabilities. Hyperactivity and impulsivity may result in behavioral issues and conflicts with peers or colleagues.

- Social and Emotional Difficulties: ADHD can affect social interactions, leading to misunderstandings, conflicts, and difficulties in forming and maintaining relationships. Emotional regulation challenges can contribute to frustration, anxiety, and low self-esteem.

- Daily Functioning: Managing everyday tasks, such as household chores, finances, and personal care, can be overwhelming, leading to stress and a sense of inadequacy.

Personalized Care and Treatment Plans

Importance of Individualized Approaches

Effective management of ADHD or ADD requires personalized care that addresses the unique needs and strengths of each individual. This approach involves a combination of strategies, including behavioral interventions, educational accommodations, and, when appropriate, medication.

Behavioral Interventions

Behavioral therapies focus on developing coping skills and strategies to manage symptoms. Cognitive-behavioral therapy (CBT) is particularly effective, helping individuals reframe negative thought patterns and develop practical solutions for daily challenges. Techniques such as time management training, organizational skills development, and mindfulness practices can enhance self-regulation and reduce symptoms.

Educational Accommodations

In academic settings, personalized accommodations are crucial for supporting students with ADHD or ADD. These may include extended time on tests, preferential seating, use of technology for organization, and individualized instruction. Collaborating with educators to create an inclusive and supportive learning environment fosters academic success and emotional well-being.

Medication

Medication can play a vital role in managing ADHD symptoms, particularly for those with significant impairment. Stimulant medications (e.g., methylphenidate and amphetamines) and non-stimulant options (e.g., atomoxetine and guanfacine) have proven effective in improving attention, reducing hyperactivity, and enhancing overall functioning. It is essential to work closely with healthcare providers to find the right medication and dosage, considering potential side effects and individual responses.

A Parent's Journey: Navigating Early Diagnosis

Emily, a mother of two, noticed early on that her son, Jack, struggled with attention and organization. While his peers easily followed classroom routines, Jack often appeared lost in his thoughts, forgetting instructions and misplacing assignments. Teachers initially labeled him as lazy or unmotivated, but Emily knew something deeper was at play.

Determined to find answers, Emily sought a comprehensive evaluation. The diagnosis of ADHD, predominantly inattentive presentation (formerly ADD), brought a mix of relief and concern. Armed with this knowledge, Emily and Jack's educators developed a tailored support plan, incorporating organizational tools and regular check-ins. Over time, Jack's confidence grew, and his academic performance improved, underscoring the importance of early detection and individualized support.

An Adult's Perspective: Embracing ADHD in the Workplace

Mark, a talented graphic designer, struggled with chronic procrastination and missed deadlines throughout his career. Despite his creativity and skill, these challenges threatened his professional growth. After a series of job changes and mounting frustration, Mark sought an evaluation and received an ADHD diagnosis at 35.

Understanding his condition allowed Mark to implement effective coping strategies. He utilized digital project management tools, broke tasks into manageable chunks, and practiced mindfulness to improve focus. Additionally, Mark advocated for flexible work arrangements with his employer, fostering a more supportive and productive work environment. His journey highlights the transformative power of self-awareness and tailored interventions in managing ADHD as an adult.

Modern Language and Practical Advice

Using Inclusive Language

Modern language that embraces neurodiversity and avoids stigmatizing terms is crucial in fostering acceptance and understanding. Referring to ADHD as a neurodevelopmental variation rather than a disorder emphasizes its place within the spectrum of human diversity. Highlighting strengths associated with ADHD, such as creativity, problem-solving abilities, and resilience, shifts the focus from deficits to potential.

Practical Advice for Managing ADHD

1. Establish Routine and Structure: Consistent daily routines help manage time and reduce overwhelm. Use planners, calendars, and digital reminders to keep track of tasks and deadlines.

2. Prioritize Self-Care: Regular exercise, balanced nutrition, and adequate sleep support overall well-being and symptom management. Incorporate stress-reducing activities such as meditation, hobbies, and social connections.

3. Seek Support: Building a support network of family, friends, and professionals provides emotional encouragement and practical assistance. Consider joining support groups or online communities to share experiences and strategies.

4. Advocate for Yourself: Effective communication with educators, employers, and healthcare providers is essential. Clearly articulate your needs and collaborate to develop accommodations and support plans that enhance your strengths and mitigate challenges.

5. Educate and Empower: Continuously educate yourself about ADHD and available resources. Empower yourself with knowledge and skills to navigate the condition confidently and advocate for systemic changes that promote inclusivity.

Understanding the link between ADHD and ADD involves recognizing their shared symptoms and unique presentations, exploring common challenges, and emphasizing the importance of personalized care. By integrating storytelling elements, modern language, and practical advice, we create a compassionate and inclusive narrative that empowers individuals with ADHD or ADD to thrive.

Through early detection, tailored interventions, and a supportive community, we can transform the journey of living with ADHD into one of resilience, self-advocacy, and potential. Embracing neurodiversity enriches our society, fostering environments where every individual can contribute their unique strengths and perspectives. As we continue to raise awareness and promote understanding, we pave the way for a more inclusive and empathetic world for those affected by ADHD

CHAPTER 6

NAVIGATING DAILY LIFE WITH ADHD: CHALLENGES, STRATEGIES, AND EMPOWERMENT

Living with Attention-Deficit/Hyperactivity Disorder (ADHD) involves navigating a unique set of challenges that affect daily functioning and overall quality of life. This narrative explores how ADHD symptoms impact individuals, identifies when these symptoms become impairing, and offers practical strategies to manage ADHD effectively through storytelling, modern language, and actionable advice.

Understanding Daily Life Impacts: The ADHD Experience

ADHD affects individuals across various facets of daily life, from academic and professional settings to personal relationships and self-care routines. Common symptoms such as inattention, impulsivity, and hyperactivity can disrupt:

- Academic Performance: Difficulty focusing in class, forgetfulness with assignments, and challenges in organizing study materials.
- Work Productivity: Procrastination, difficulty meeting deadlines, and inconsistent performance at work.
- Interpersonal Relationships: Impulsive reactions, forgetfulness in social commitments, and challenges in maintaining friendships or romantic partnerships.

In addition to these challenges, individuals with ADHD may struggle with time management, organization, and emotional regulation, impacting their ability to maintain routines and cope with everyday stressors. When these symptoms significantly impair functioning and persist across multiple settings (e.g., home, school, work), ADHD becomes a clinical disorder that warrants professional evaluation and intervention.

Identifying Clinical Impairment: When ADHD Requires Intervention

ADHD becomes clinically impairing when symptoms interfere with an individual's ability to meet developmental milestones, academic expectations, occupational demands, or social responsibilities. Symptoms must be persistent, pervasive, and disproportionate to developmental level or chronological age to meet diagnostic criteria.

Early identification and intervention are crucial to minimizing long-term impacts on academic achievement, self-esteem, and mental health. Seeking professional evaluation from a healthcare provider experienced in ADHD assessment ensures accurate diagnosis and tailored treatment planning that addresses individual strengths and challenges.

Strategies for Managing ADHD Symptoms: Optimizing Daily Routines

Managing ADHD involves adopting strategies that enhance organization, time management, and emotional regulation. Practical advice includes:

- Creating Structured Routines: Establishing daily schedules with designated times for tasks, breaks, and relaxation promotes consistency and reduces procrastination.
- Utilizing Organization Tools: Using planners, digital apps, and reminder systems helps individuals track deadlines, appointments, and commitments.

- Breaking Tasks into Manageable Steps: Breaking down larger tasks into smaller, actionable steps facilitates focus and reduces overwhelm.

- Implementing Behavioral Strategies: Employing strategies such as the Pomodoro Technique (work intervals followed by short breaks) enhances productivity and maintains attention.

Storytelling elements enrich this narrative by sharing personal experiences of individuals overcoming daily challenges associated with ADHD. These stories illustrate resilience, creativity in problem-solving, and the transformative impact of adopting effective coping strategies.

Modern Language and Practical Advice: Empowering Individuals with ADHD

Using modern language that emphasizes strengths and adaptive strategies fosters a positive self-concept and reduces stigma associated with ADHD. Encouraging self-advocacy involves educating oneself about ADHD, communicating openly with healthcare providers, and seeking support from peers and community resources.

In conclusion, navigating daily life with ADHD involves acknowledging challenges, implementing effective strategies, and seeking support to optimize functioning and enhance quality of life. By embracing individual differences and promoting inclusive environments, we empower individuals with ADHD to thrive and contribute meaningfully to their communities.

CHAPTER 7

ADULTS WITH ADHD: EMBRACING CHALLENGES AND EMPOWERING GROWTH

Navigating life as an adult with Attention-Deficit/Hyperactivity Disorder (ADHD) presents unique challenges that impact personal, professional, and social spheres. This narrative explores the distinct struggles faced by adults with ADHD, offers strategies for managing disorganization, and emphasizes self-acceptance and empowerment through storytelling, modern language, and practical advice.

Addressing Unique Struggles: The Adult ADHD Experience

For adults with ADHD, managing daily responsibilities, maintaining focus, and staying organized can present significant challenges. Common struggles include:

- Time Management: Difficulty prioritizing tasks, meeting deadlines, and estimating time accurately.

- Organization: Challenges in maintaining tidy spaces, keeping track of belongings, and managing paperwork.

- Impulsivity: Making impulsive decisions in finances, relationships, or career choices without fully considering consequences.

- Emotional Regulation: Difficulty managing emotions, leading to mood swings, frustration, or hypersensitivity in social interactions.

These challenges can impact relationships, career advancement, financial stability, and overall well-being. Adults with ADHD may also face feelings of inadequacy, self-doubt, and frustration due to perceived failures in meeting societal expectations.

Strategies for Coping with Disorganization: Thriving at Home and Work

Managing disorganization involves implementing practical strategies tailored to individual strengths and challenges:

- Setting Clear Goals: Establishing achievable goals and breaking them down into manageable tasks enhances focus and motivation.
- Creating Structure: Using visual aids, such as calendars, to-do lists, and reminder apps, helps maintain routines and track deadlines.
- Decluttering Spaces: Simplifying environments at home and in the workplace reduces distractions and promotes productivity.
- Time-Blocking: Allocating specific time blocks for different tasks increases efficiency and reduces procrastination.

Employing these strategies requires persistence and experimentation to find what works best for each individual. Embracing a growth mindset and celebrating small victories fosters resilience and motivates continued self-improvement.

Promoting Self-Acceptance and Empowerment: Embracing ADHD as a Unique Trait

Promoting self-acceptance involves reframing ADHD as a neurodevelopmental trait with strengths and challenges:

- Recognizing Strengths: Emphasizing creativity, problem-solving skills, spontaneity, and hyperfocus as valuable assets in personal and professional endeavors.

- Building Support Networks: Connecting with peers, support groups, and mentors who understand ADHD fosters understanding, empathy, and practical advice.

- Seeking Professional Support: Consulting healthcare providers, therapists, or ADHD coaches for personalized strategies and therapeutic interventions.

Storytelling elements enrich this narrative by sharing personal journeys of resilience, adaptation, and growth. These stories illustrate how individuals with ADHD navigate challenges, embrace their unique traits, and find success in diverse fields and personal pursuits.

Modern Language and Practical Advice: Empowering Adults with ADHD

Using modern language that emphasizes strengths and adaptive strategies reduces stigma and promotes self-confidence. Practical advice includes advocating for workplace accommodations, setting realistic expectations, and practicing self-care to manage stress and maintain well-being.

In conclusion, adults with ADHD navigate unique challenges with resilience and creativity. By embracing self-acceptance, implementing effective strategies, and seeking support from peers and professionals, individuals with ADHD can thrive in all aspects of life and contribute meaningfully to their communities.

CHAPTER 8

THRIVING WITH ADHD: UNLEASHING POTENTIAL AND EMBRACING SUCCESS

Living with Attention-Deficit/Hyperactivity Disorder (ADHD) presents unique challenges, but it also offers opportunities for growth, creativity, and success. This narrative explores strategies for maximizing potential, achieving success in work and relationships, navigating social interactions, and reducing chaos through storytelling, modern language, and practical advice.

Tips for Maximizing Life with ADHD: Strategies for Success

Achieving success with ADHD involves harnessing strengths and implementing effective strategies:

- Play to Your Strengths: Embrace creativity, spontaneity, and hyperfocus as assets that fuel innovation and problem-solving.

- Set Clear Goals: Establish specific, achievable goals and break them down into actionable steps to maintain focus and motivation.

- Utilize Visual Aids: Use calendars, to-do lists, reminder apps, and organizational tools to manage time, tasks, and commitments.

- Prioritize Self-Care: Maintain a balanced lifestyle with regular exercise, adequate sleep, healthy nutrition, and mindfulness practices to support mental well-being.

These strategies empower individuals to leverage their strengths and overcome challenges, fostering resilience and enhancing overall quality of life.

Navigating Social Interactions: Managing Communication Challenges

Effective communication is key to navigating social interactions with ADHD:

- Active Listening: Practice active listening techniques, such as summarizing and paraphrasing, to ensure understanding in conversations.

- Clarify and Confirm: Ask clarifying questions and confirm details to avoid misunderstandings and enhance communication clarity.

- Use Visual Cues: Employ visual aids, gestures, and facial expressions to supplement verbal communication and convey meaning effectively.

- Manage Impulsivity: Pause before responding impulsively, allowing time to process information and consider responses thoughtfully.

Building strong relationships involves empathy, patience, and mutual understanding. Sharing personal anecdotes of overcoming communication challenges through adaptation and learning enriches this narrative, illustrating growth and resilience in social settings.

Strategies for Decreasing Chaos: Achieving Harmony in Life

Reducing chaos involves implementing organizational strategies in various life domains:

- Home Environment: Establish routines for cleaning and organizing spaces, designate storage areas for belongings, and declutter regularly.

- Workplace: Prioritize tasks, set deadlines, and utilize time-management techniques like the Pomodoro Technique to enhance productivity.

- Relationships: Communicate openly with partners and family members about ADHD-related challenges, collaborate on household responsibilities, and seek support from loved ones.

Storytelling elements bring these strategies to life, sharing personal experiences of individuals who have successfully navigated chaos and discord to achieve balance and harmony in their lives.

Modern Language and Practical Advice: Empowering Success with ADHD

Using modern language that celebrates neurodiversity and emphasizes adaptive strategies promotes self-acceptance and reduces stigma. Practical advice includes advocating for workplace accommodations, seeking professional support, and joining support groups or online communities to connect with peers facing similar challenges.

In conclusion, thriving with ADHD involves embracing strengths, implementing effective strategies, and nurturing supportive relationships. By fostering resilience, self-awareness, and growth mindset, individuals with ADHD can maximize their potential, achieve success in diverse areas of life, and contribute meaningfully to their communities.

CHAPTER 9

UNLEASHING INNER TALENTS AND STRENGTHS: EMBRACING THE POWER OF ADHD

Living with Attention-Deficit/Hyperactivity Disorder (ADHD) often brings challenges, but it also offers a wealth of untapped potential and unique strengths. This narrative explores the importance of identifying and cultivating individual talents, recognizing the strengths associated with ADHD traits, and promoting self-discovery and self-expression as pathways to embracing neurodiversity.

Encouraging Individuals to Identify and Cultivate Their Unique Talents

Every individual possesses unique talents and abilities waiting to be discovered and nurtured. For individuals with ADHD, this process begins with self-awareness and exploration:

- Identifying Passions: Reflect on activities that bring joy, excitement, and a sense of accomplishment. Whether it's creative arts, problem-solving, or hands-on projects, identifying passions provides a foundation for talent development.

- Exploring Diverse Interests: Experiment with different hobbies, skills, and areas of interest to uncover hidden talents and strengths. ADHD often fosters curiosity and adaptability, making exploration a natural pathway to personal growth.

- Seeking Feedback: Solicit feedback from trusted peers, mentors, and educators to gain insight into strengths and areas for growth. Constructive feedback helps refine talents and build confidence in abilities.

By encouraging individuals to explore their passions and invest time in activities that align with their interests, we empower them to harness their full potential and thrive.

Recognizing the Strengths Associated with ADHD Traits

ADHD traits such as creativity, hyperfocus, and resilience contribute to a unique set of strengths that can be leveraged in various aspects of life.

- Creativity: ADHD often sparks innovative thinking, outside-the-box problem-solving, and artistic expression. Embracing creativity fosters ingenuity and opens doors to new opportunities.
- Hyperfocus: While ADHD is characterized by difficulties in maintaining attention, hyperfocus on tasks of high interest or importance can lead to exceptional productivity and achievement.
- Resilience: Overcoming challenges associated with ADHD builds resilience, determination, and adaptability. Individuals learn to persevere in the face of adversity and develop strategies for personal growth.

By reframing ADHD traits as strengths rather than limitations, individuals gain a renewed sense of self-worth and confidence in their abilities.

Promoting Self-Discovery and Self-Expression: Embracing Neurodiversity

Self-discovery involves embracing one's unique neurodivergent traits and celebrating individuality.

- Self-Reflection: Engage in introspective practices such as journaling, mindfulness, or therapy to explore personal strengths, values, and aspirations.

- Self-Expression: Express creativity and emotions through artistic outlets, writing, music, or other forms of self-expression. Artistic endeavors provide a platform for self-discovery and communication.

Community Engagement: Connect with neurodiverse communities, support groups, or advocacy organizations to share experiences, gain perspective, and cultivate a sense of belonging.

Storytelling elements enrich this narrative by sharing personal journeys of individuals who have embraced their ADHD traits, discovered their unique talents, and achieved personal and professional fulfillment. These stories inspire empathy, foster understanding, and celebrate the diversity of human experience.

Embracing Neurodiversity: Celebrating Individuality and Potential

Embracing neurodiversity involves promoting a culture of acceptance, inclusion, and appreciation for diverse cognitive styles and abilities:

- Education and Awareness: Educate oneself and others about ADHD, challenging stereotypes, and promoting understanding of neurodivergent experiences.

- Advocacy and Support: Advocate for inclusive policies, accommodations, and support services that empower individuals with ADHD to thrive in educational, professional, and social environments.

- Empowerment: Encourage self-advocacy and empowerment by providing resources, mentorship, and opportunities for individuals to advocate for their needs and contribute to community dialogue.

Unleashing inner talents and strengths involves embracing ADHD traits as unique assets, fostering self-discovery through exploration and self-expression, and promoting a culture of neurodiversity acceptance. By celebrating individuality and potential, we cultivate a society where every person can contribute their talents, perspectives, and creativity to create a brighter future for all.

CHAPTER 10

ACHIEVING BALANCE AND SELF-REFLECTION: NAVIGATING LIFE WITH ADHD

Living with Attention-Deficit/Hyperactivity Disorder (ADHD) involves a journey of self-discovery, embracing strengths, addressing challenges, and achieving balance in various aspects of life. This narrative explores strategies for leveraging strengths, encouraging self-reflection, and cultivating a positive self-image while navigating the unique traits of ADHD through storytelling, modern language, and practical advice.

Strategies for Achieving Balance: Leveraging Strengths and Addressing Weaknesses

Achieving balance in life with ADHD requires a holistic approach that acknowledges both strengths and challenges:

- Identifying Strengths: Recognize and capitalize on ADHD-related strengths such as creativity, hyperfocus, and resilience. These traits can be harnessed to excel in academic, professional, and personal pursuits.
- Addressing Weaknesses: Implement strategies such as organization techniques, time management skills, and behavioral therapies to mitigate challenges associated with ADHD symptoms.
- Creating Structure: Establish daily routines, prioritize tasks, and set realistic goals to maintain consistency and reduce stress.

- Seeking Support: Build a support network of family, friends, educators, and healthcare professionals who understand ADHD and can provide guidance, encouragement, and practical assistance.

By leveraging strengths and implementing targeted strategies, individuals with ADHD can optimize their potential and achieve a balanced, fulfilling life.

Encouraging Self-Reflection and Self-Improvement

Self-reflection is a powerful tool for personal growth and development:

- Mindfulness Practices: Engage in mindfulness meditation, deep breathing exercises, or yoga to cultivate self-awareness, reduce impulsivity, and enhance focus.
- Journaling: Maintain a journal to reflect on daily experiences, identify patterns of behavior, and set intentions for self-improvement.
- Goal Setting: Establish short-term and long-term goals that align with personal values and aspirations. Break goals into manageable steps and track progress to maintain motivation.
- Learning from Setbacks: Embrace failures and setbacks as opportunities for learning and growth. Analyze challenges, identify strategies for improvement, and celebrate achievements along the way.

Self-reflection fosters resilience, enhances decision-making skills, and promotes emotional well-being, empowering individuals to navigate life's challenges with confidence.

Cultivating a Positive Self-Image: Embracing Identity with ADHD

Cultivating a positive self-image involves embracing one's identity with ADHD and celebrating unique traits:

- Self-Acceptance: Embrace ADHD as a part of one's identity, recognizing that neurodiversity contributes to diverse perspectives and strengths.
- Building Confidence: Focus on personal achievements, strengths, and capabilities. Celebrate successes, no matter how small, and acknowledge efforts made toward personal growth.
- Education and Advocacy: Educate oneself and others about ADHD, challenge stereotypes, and advocate for inclusive environments that celebrate neurodiversity.

Storytelling elements enrich this narrative by sharing personal anecdotes of individuals who have embraced their ADHD identity, overcome challenges, and achieved personal and professional success. These stories inspire hope, foster empathy, and illustrate the transformative power of self-acceptance.

Modern Language and Practical Advice: Empowering Balance and Growth

- Using modern language that celebrates strengths and promotes resilience reduces stigma and fosters a supportive community:
- Practical Advice: Implement organizational tools, time-management strategies, and self-care routines to optimize daily functioning and reduce stress.

- Community Engagement: Connect with neurodiverse communities, support groups, or online forums to share experiences, gain support, and exchange practical advice.

Achieving balance and self-reflection involves leveraging strengths, addressing challenges, and cultivating a positive self-image while navigating life with ADHD. By embracing neurodiversity, fostering self-acceptance, and seeking support, individuals with ADHD can thrive, contribute meaningfully, and inspire others within their communities.

CHAPTER 11

PRACTICAL TOOLS FOR ORGANIZATION AND MEMORY ENHANCEMENT: EMPOWERING INDIVIDUALS WITH ADHD

Living with Attention-Deficit/Hyperactivity Disorder (ADHD) often involves navigating challenges related to organization and memory. This narrative offers a comprehensive guide for individuals with ADHD, providing tips to improve organization, create effective systems and routines, and enhance memory through storytelling, modern language, and practical advice.

Improving Organization: Creating Effective Systems and Routines

Organizational challenges are common among individuals with ADHD, impacting various aspects of daily life. Effective strategies include:

- Utilizing Visual Tools: Implement visual aids such as calendars, planners, whiteboards, and sticky notes to track tasks, appointments, and deadlines.

- Setting Clear Goals: Establish specific, achievable goals and break them down into smaller, manageable tasks. Prioritize tasks based on importance and deadlines.

- Creating Structured Routines: Develop daily routines for waking up, meal times, work/study sessions, exercise, and bedtime to promote consistency and reduce impulsivity.

- Decluttering and Simplifying Spaces: Organize work and living spaces by categorizing items, utilizing storage solutions, and minimizing distractions to enhance focus and productivity.

Personal anecdotes and storytelling illustrate how individuals have transformed their organizational habits, overcome challenges, and achieved success in various domains. These stories inspire empathy, offer practical insights, and highlight the transformative impact of implementing effective organizational strategies.

Memory Enhancement Techniques: Tailored Approaches for ADHD

Memory difficulties can pose significant challenges for individuals with ADHD. Tailored techniques include

- Chunking Information: Break down information into smaller chunks or categories to enhance retention and recall.
- Utilizing Mnemonic Devices: Employ mnemonic devices, acronyms, rhymes, or visual imagery to aid memory retrieval.
- Repetition and Review: Review information regularly through spaced repetition techniques to reinforce learning and improve retention.
- Utilizing External Memory Aids: Use technology such as reminder apps, alarms, voice memos, and digital organizers to prompt memory recall and manage daily tasks.

By incorporating these memory enhancement techniques into daily routines, individuals with ADHD can improve information processing, recall accuracy, and overall cognitive functioning.

Modern Language and Practical Advice: Empowering Action and Growth

Using modern language that emphasizes strengths and fosters resilience reduces stigma and promotes self-empowerment:

Practical Tips: Implement organizational tools and memory techniques gradually, experimenting with different strategies to identify what works best.

- Self-Advocacy: Advocate for workplace accommodations, educational support, and personalized strategies that align with individual needs and preferences.
- Community Engagement: Connect with peers, support groups, or online communities to share experiences, gain insights, and access resources for ongoing support.

Practical tools for organization and memory enhancement empower individuals with ADHD to navigate daily challenges, achieve personal goals, and thrive in various aspects of life. By embracing adaptive strategies, fostering self-awareness, and seeking support, individuals with ADHD can optimize their potential and contribute meaningfully to their communities.

CHAPTER 12

OVERCOMING PROCRASTINATION, CLUTTER, AND FORGETFULNESS: STRATEGIES FOR SUCCESS WITH ADHD

Living with Attention-Deficit/Hyperactivity Disorder (ADHD) often involves grappling with challenges such as procrastination, clutter, and forgetfulness. This narrative explores effective strategies for managing these common hurdles, offers tips to create an organized environment, and provides memory aids tailored to enhance daily functioning through storytelling, modern language, and practical advice.

Strategies for Managing Procrastination and Forgetfulness

Procrastination and forgetfulness are frequent obstacles for individuals with ADHD, impacting productivity and daily routines. Effective strategies include:

- Breaking Tasks into Smaller Steps: Divide tasks into manageable chunks to reduce overwhelm and increase motivation.

- Setting Clear Deadlines: Establish realistic deadlines and use visual reminders such as alarms or digital planners to stay on track.

- Implementing Time-Management Techniques: Utilize techniques like the Pomodoro Technique (work intervals followed by short breaks) to maintain focus and productivity.

- Practicing Mindfulness: Incorporate mindfulness practices such as deep breathing or meditation to improve self-awareness and reduce impulsivity.

Personal anecdotes and storytelling illustrate how individuals have overcome procrastination and developed effective time-management habits. These stories inspire empathy, provide practical insights, and highlight the transformative impact of proactive strategies.

Tips for Decluttering and Creating an Organized Environment

Clutter can exacerbate distractions and hinder productivity. Practical tips for creating an organized environment include:

- Designating Spaces: Assign specific areas for work, study, and relaxation to maintain clear boundaries and minimize distractions.
- Implementing Storage Solutions: Use bins, shelves, and organizers to categorize and store belongings, reducing visual and mental clutter.
- Regular Decluttering: Schedule regular sessions to sort through items, discard unnecessary items, and organize remaining belongings.
- Streamlining Digital Spaces: Organize digital files, emails, and desktop icons into folders to enhance digital organization and accessibility.

Storytelling elements enrich this narrative by sharing personal journeys of individuals who have transformed cluttered spaces into organized sanctuaries, enhancing productivity and mental clarity. These stories inspire motivation, offer practical guidance, and underscore the importance of creating supportive environments.

Memory Aids and Techniques to Combat Forgetfulness

Forgetfulness can pose challenges in managing tasks, appointments, and commitments. Memory aids and techniques include:

- Utilizing Visual Reminders: Place sticky notes, visual schedules, or checklists in prominent locations to prompt memory recall.
- Digital Tools: Use reminder apps, calendar alerts, and voice memos on smartphones or tablets to set alarms and notifications for important tasks.
- Association Techniques: Link new information with familiar cues or create mnemonic devices to aid memory retention and retrieval
- Daily Review: Establish a routine for reviewing daily schedules, tasks, and upcoming events to reinforce memory recall and prevent oversights.

By incorporating memory aids into daily routines and environments, individuals with ADHD can enhance cognitive functioning, improve task management, and reduce the impact of forgetfulness on daily life.

Modern Language and Practical Advice: Empowering Action and Growth

Using modern language that celebrates progress and promotes resilience fosters a positive mindset and reduces self-criticism:

- Practical Implementation: Start with small changes and gradually incorporate new strategies to build habits that support organization and memory.

- Self-Reflection: Reflect on successes and challenges, identify areas for improvement, and adjust strategies accordingly to optimize effectiveness.
- Community Support: Connect with peers, support groups, or online communities to share experiences, gain insights, and access resources for ongoing support.

In conclusion, overcoming procrastination, clutter, and forgetfulness involves adopting proactive strategies, creating supportive environments, and utilizing memory aids tailored to individual needs. By embracing resilience, fostering self-awareness, and seeking support, individuals with ADHD can navigate challenges effectively, achieve personal goals, and thrive in their daily lives.

CONCLUSION

EMBRACING UNIQUENESS AND ADVOCATING FOR ADHD AWARENESS

Throughout this exploration of living with Attention-Deficit/Hyperactivity Disorder (ADHD), we've uncovered valuable insights, practical strategies, and empowering narratives that highlight the resilience and potential of individuals with ADHD. This conclusion summarizes key takeaways, empowers individuals to embrace their uniqueness, and advocates for greater awareness, understanding, and support for those living with ADHD.

Summarizing Key Insights and Takeaways

1. Strengths and Challenges: ADHD is characterized by unique strengths such as creativity, hyperfocus, and resilience, alongside challenges in organization, time management, and impulsivity.

2. Personal Growth: Embracing ADHD involves recognizing individual strengths, fostering self-awareness, and implementing strategies that optimize personal and professional success.

3. Community and Support: Building a supportive network of peers, mentors, healthcare professionals, and community resources is crucial for empowerment and ongoing growth.

4. Education and Advocacy: Advocating for inclusive environments, educational accommodations, and workplace support enhances opportunities and reduces stigma associated with ADHD.

5. Holistic Well-Being: Prioritizing self-care, maintaining balanced lifestyles, and utilizing mindfulness practices contribute to overall well-being and resilience.

Empowering Individuals with ADHD to Thrive

Empowerment begins with self-acceptance and celebrating neurodiversity:

- Self-Discovery: Encourage individuals to explore their passions, talents, and interests, leveraging ADHD traits to excel in their chosen endeavors.
- Resilience and Adaptability: Highlight stories of individuals who have overcome challenges, embraced their uniqueness, and achieved personal and professional success.
- Advocacy: Equip individuals with tools and knowledge to advocate for their needs, access resources, and promote greater understanding of ADHD within their communities.

By fostering a positive mindset, embracing strengths, and seeking support, individuals with ADHD can unlock their full potential and thrive in all aspects of life.

Advocating for Greater Awareness and Support

1. Education and Awareness: Promote accurate information about ADHD, challenge stereotypes, and educate the public, educators, and employers about the diverse experiences and strengths of individuals with ADHD.

2. Policy and Accessibility: Advocate for policies that support neurodiversity, ensure accessibility to accommodations in educational and workplace settings, and promote inclusivity.

3. Community Engagement: Engage with advocacy organizations, support groups, and healthcare providers to foster a supportive environment and amplify the voices of individuals with ADHD.

4. Research and Innovation: Support research initiatives that advance understanding, treatment options, and support systems for individuals living with ADHD.

By raising awareness, promoting acceptance, and advocating for inclusive practices, we can create a more supportive and equitable society for individuals with ADHD.

In conclusion, living with ADHD presents unique challenges and opportunities for personal growth and achievement. By embracing strengths, implementing effective strategies, and advocating for greater awareness and support, individuals with ADHD can navigate life's complexities with resilience, achieve their goals, and contribute meaningfully to their communities. Together, let us continue to empower and uplift individuals with ADHD, fostering a world where every person is valued for their unique abilities and contributions.